is for Running

A Primer for the Footsore

by

Ray Charbonneau

Second Edition

ISBN-13: 978-1-4663-5763-1
ISBN-10: 1-4663-5763-0

Design: Y42K Book Production Services: y42k.com

Also by Ray Charbonneau:
Chasing the Runner's High
Overthinking the Marathon

Edited by Ray Charbonneau:
The 27th Mile

For more information, please visit http://www.y42k.com

R is also for Ruth,
on the occasion of her second marathon

Ray Charbonneau

A is for AGE
The younger the faster
But sooner or later
You become an old bastard

Ray Charbonneau

B is for BEER
Drink after the race
A little too much and
You'll fall on your face

C is for CARBO-LOADING
Push back the wall
By cooking up pasta
And eating it all

Ray Charbonneau

D is for DNF
Quit 'fore the end
A shrug of your shoulders
Then go home to mend

Ray Charbonneau

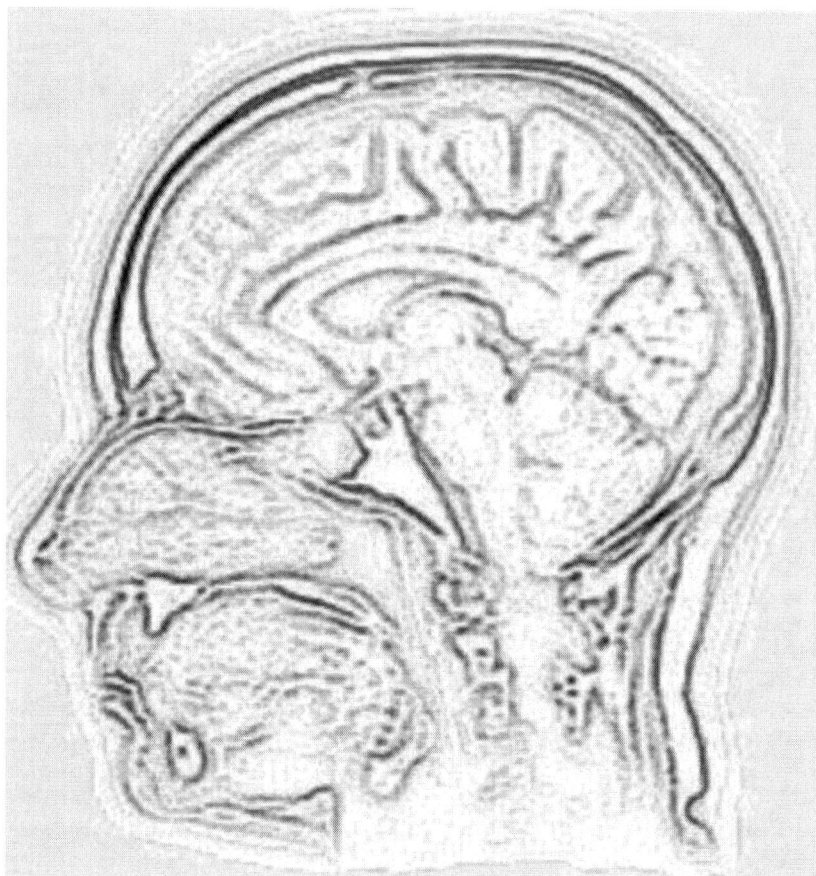

E is for ENDORPHINS
The runner's high
They're what we're all chasing
One answer to "why"

F is for FINISH
The end of the run
A prize when you get there
Makes it more fun

Ray Charbonneau

G is for GLOBAL POSITIONING SYSTEM
It shows where you are
And when you're done running
It tells you how far

Ray Charbonneau

H is for HILLS
Run up, then run down
Do plenty of climbing
To earn you a crown

I is for INJURY
Not much you can do
Sooner or later
One'll happen to you

J is for JOGGING
You're still on the go
It's just like you're running
But a little more slow

K is for KICK
At the end of the race
If you want to win something
Better pick up the pace

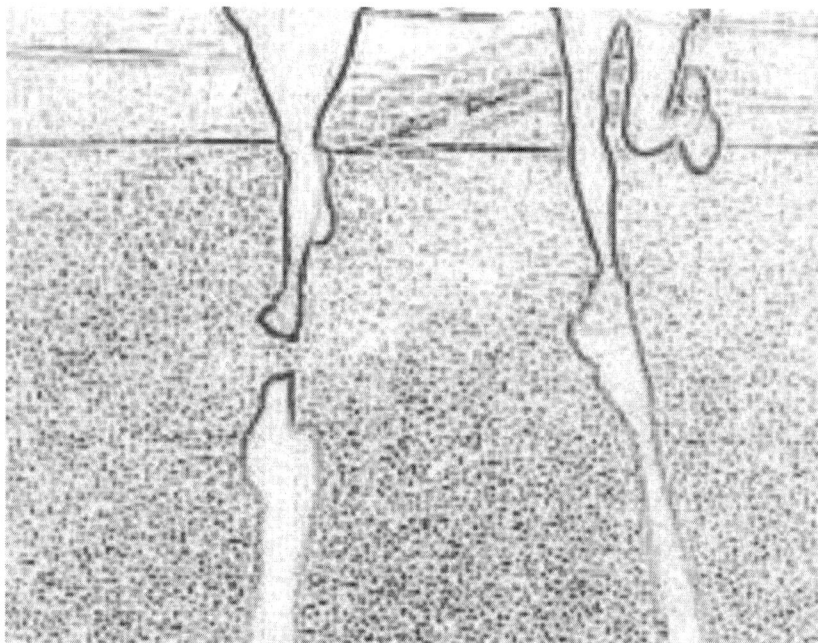

L is for LONG RUN
Usually done slow
The easier you run them
The further you go

M is for MARATHON
A test of your heart
The first 20 miles
Is only the start

N is for NUMBER
Pin one on your chest
So races can tell
Your time from the rest

Ray Charbonneau

O is for OUTDOORS
The place where you run
Trudging on treadmills
Just isn't as fun

Ray Charbonneau

P is for PORTAPOTTIES
There isn't much time
You've had too much water
So get into line

Ray Charbonneau

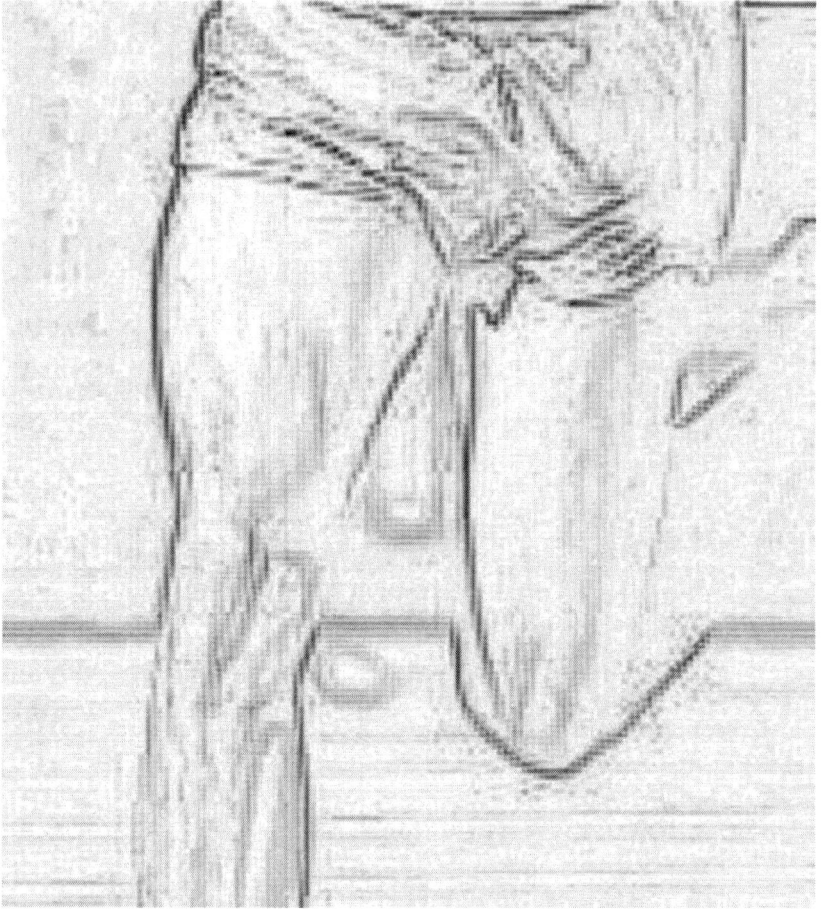

Q is for QUADRICEPS
In front of the thigh
If they get too tired
You're going to die

Ray Charbonneau

R is for REST
A day with no run
Do some cross-training
Or lie in the sun

S is for SINGLET
The shirt for thinclads
It bears your club logo
And leaves a weird tan

T is for TROPHY
Win one at the race
Who cares if it's tiny
And labeled "Third Place"

U is for ULTRAS
A test of your will
If it weren't for the finish
You'd be out there still

V is for VO2MAX
What does it mean?
Your oxygen usage
Higher is keen

Ray Charbonneau

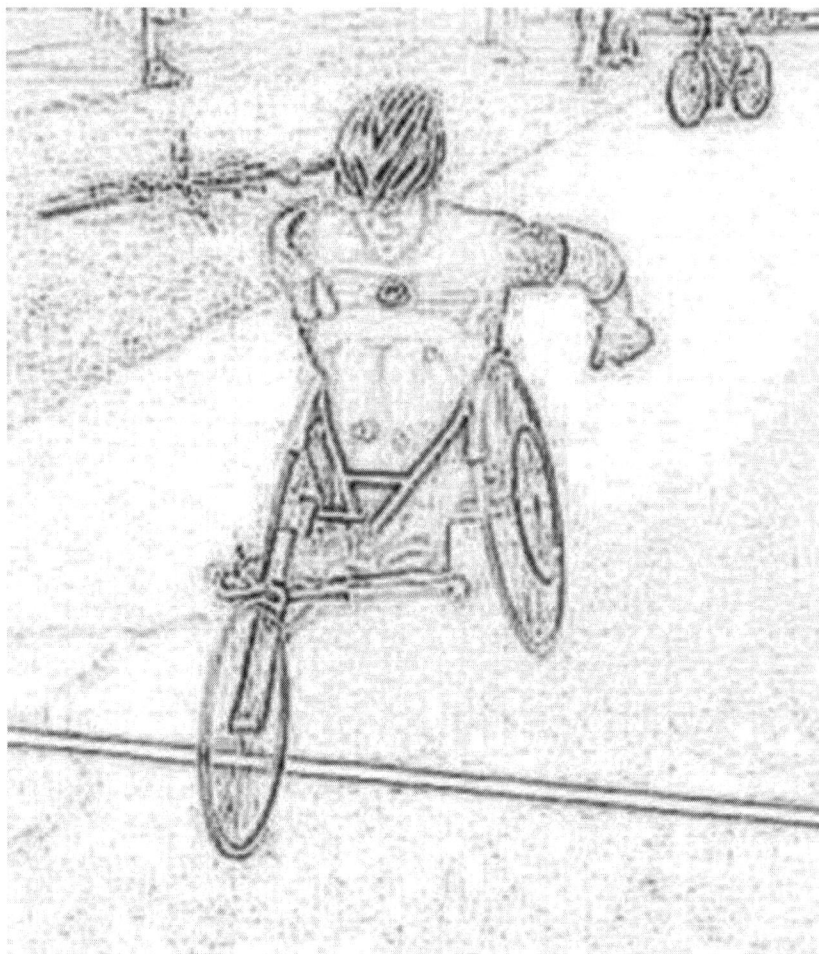

W is for WINNING
The reason we race
But only one person
Ends up in first place

X is for XXL
Shirts come in that size
They fit onto Clydesdales
With Kenyans for thighs

Y is for YASSO 800s
Don't run them sedately
For runners of Bart's age
You call them 880s

Ray Charbonneau

Z is for ZEN
The miles we schlep?
A journey of thousands
Begins with a step

About the author:

Ray Charbonneau lives in Arlington, MA with his wife and their two cats. You can often find Ray and Ruth out on the streets running, but Felix and Phoebe stay inside.

Ray is also the author of *Overthinking the Marathon* and *Chasing the Runner's High: My Sixty Million-Step Program* and the editor of *The 27th Mile*. His stories and articles have appeared in national dead-tree publications and landfill-saving electronic formats.

Find out more at www.y42k.com

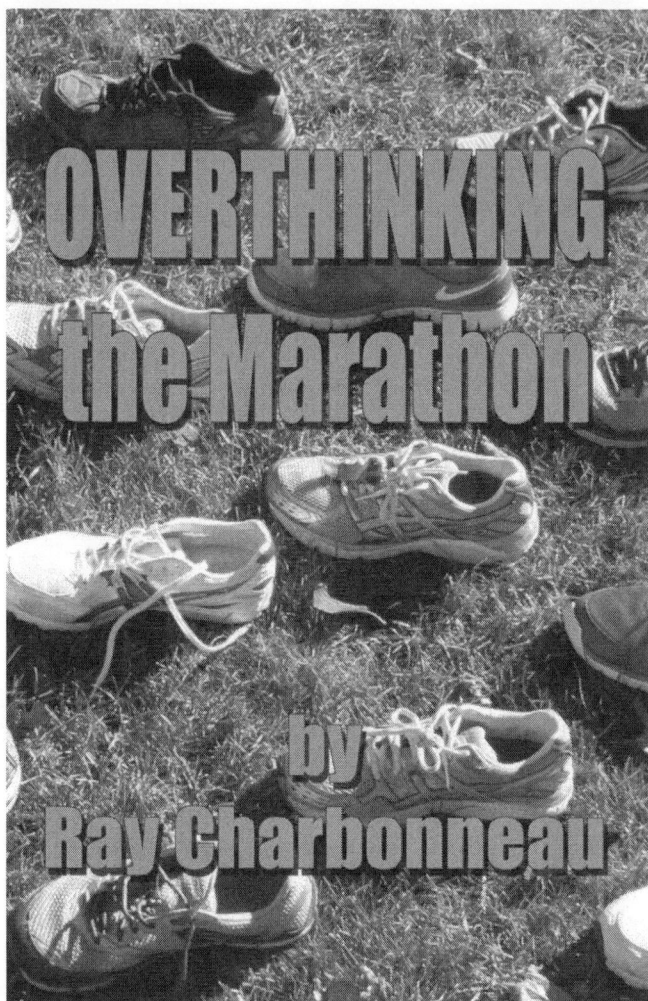

Overthinking the Marathon
"You couldn't find a better training partner as you get ready for
your next 26.2-miler." – Amby Burfoot
$12.99 paperback / $2.99 ebook
More info at y42k.com

Chasing the Runner's High
"A hard look at the mind of a runner" – Marshall Ulrich
$12.99 paperback / $2.99 ebook
More info at y42k.com

Interested in publishing your own book?

I can help you design and publish your book quickly, professionally, and at a low cost. Unlike other services that automate the process, I'll work directly with you every step of the way to ensure you get the book you want.

For more information, visit the Y42K Book Production Services page at:

http://www.y42k.com/bookproduction.html

6775052R00037

Made in the USA
San Bernardino, CA
14 December 2013